60
Great Solos
for
Low Voice

CREATIVELY ARRANGED BY

Tom Fettke

lillenas
PUBLISHING COMPANY

PO Box 419527
Kansas City, MO 64141

Think About His Love

Words and Music by
WALT HARRAH
Arranged by Tom Fettke

Shout to the Lord

Words and Music by
DARLENE ZSCHECH
Arranged by Tom Fettke

8

Wonderful, Wonderful Jesus

ANNA B. RUSSELL

ERNEST O. SELLERS
Arranged by Tom Fettke

Go Light Your World

Words and Music by
CHRIS RICE

18

O Lord, Most Holy

KEN BIBLE

CÉSAR FRANCK
Arranged by Tom Fettke

20

22

The Great Divide

Words and Music by
GRANT CUNNINGHAM
and MATT HUESMANN

With quiet confidence ♩ = ca. 68

1. Si - lence: try'n' to fath - om the
(2.) faith - ful, on my own I'm un -

dis - tance, look - ing out 'cross the can - yon carved by
a - ble– He found me hope - less, a - lone and sent a

way was made___ to reach the oth - er side. The

mer - cy of___ the Fa - ther cost His Son His life;___ His

love is___ deep,___ His love is___ wide,___ There's a cross

1 decresc.

to bridge the great___ di - vide. 2. God is

28

29

Mercy Saw Me

Words and Music by
GERON and BECKY DAVIS
Arranged by Tom Fettke

We Shall See Jesus

Words and Music by
DIANE WILKINSON
Arranged by Tom Fettke

Once, on a hill - side, peo - ple were gath - ered, Watch-ing as Je - sus was cru - ci - fied; No one showed mer - cy to the one who had healed them, Yet Je - sus loved

rose to the heav - ens And gave them His prom -

ise to come back a - gain. We shall see

slight accel. and cresc. *ff*

a little faster ♩ = ca. 80

Je - sus, just as they saw Him,

There is no great - er prom - ise than

Awesome God

with
How Great Is He

Words and Music by
RICH MULLINS
Arranged by Tom Fettke

44

46

Wherever He Leads I'll Go

with

Where He Leads Me

Words and Music by
B.B. McKINNEY
Arranged by Tom Fettke

*"Where He Leads Me"
Freely

*Words by E. W. Blandy; Music by John S. Norris.Arr. © 1999 by Pilot Point Music (ASCAP). All rights reserved. Administered by The Copyright Company, 40 Music Square East, Nashville, TN 37203.

52

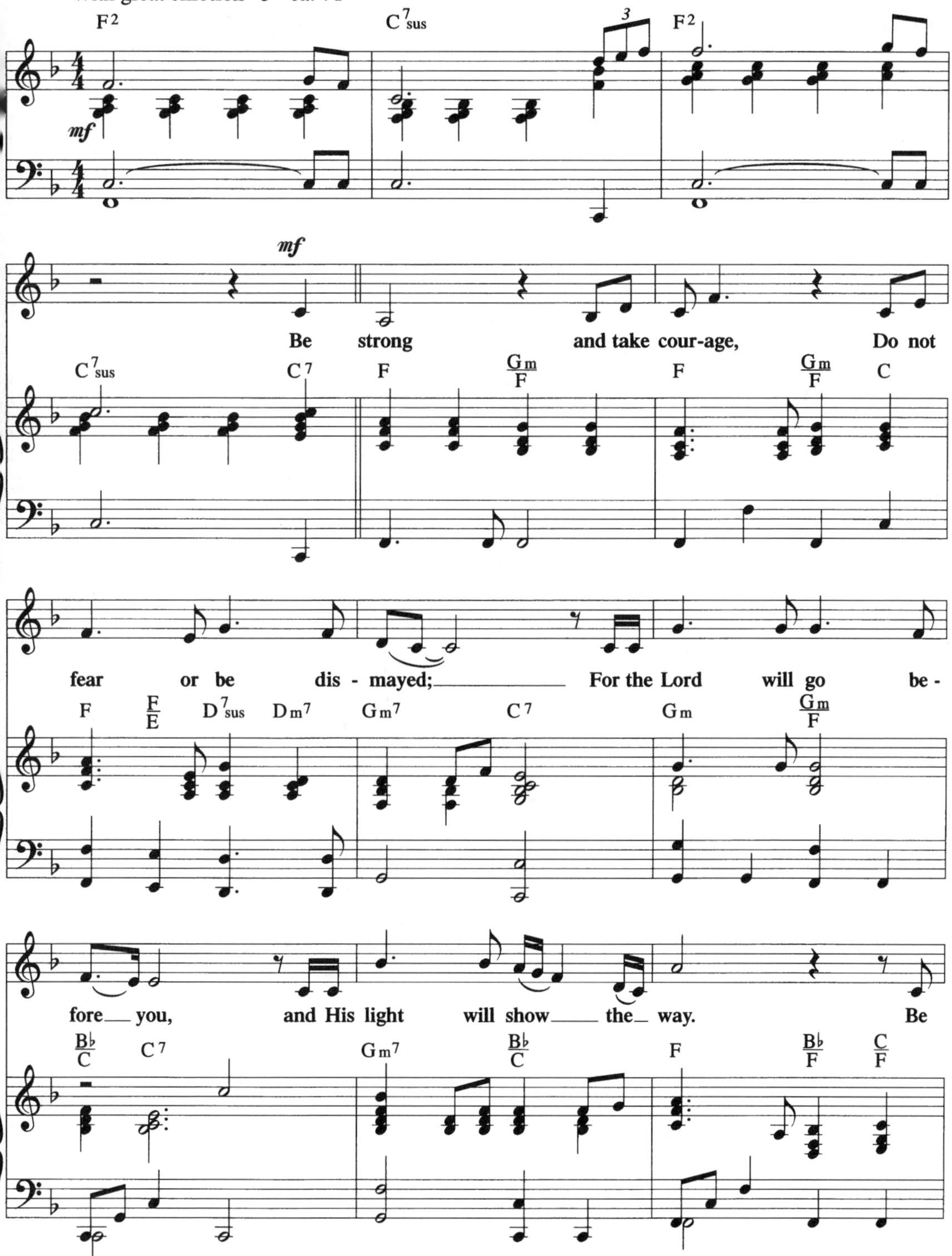

Be Strong and Take Courage

Words and Music by
BASIL CHIASSON
Arranged by Tom Fettke

With great emotion ♩ = ca. 71

F2
C7sus
F2
mf
C7sus
C7
mf
Be strong and take cour-age, Do not
F
Gm/F
F
Gm/F
C
fear or be dis - mayed;
For the Lord will go be -
F
F/E
D7sus
Dm7
Gm7
C7
Gm
Gm/F
fore you, and His light will show the way. Be
Bb/C
C7
Gm7
Bb/C
F
Bb/F
C/F

In His Presence

Words and Music by
DICK and MELODIE TUNNEY

58

He Knows Just What I Need

Words and Music by
MOSIE LISTER
Arranged by Tom Fettke

Heal Our Land

with
America, the Beautiful

Words and Music by
TOM and ROBIN BROOKS
Arranged by Tom Fettke

1. If my peo - ple will
(2. Lord, we) bow our knee, we

hum - ble them-selves,   hum - ble them-selves   and   pray;   If   they
hum - ble our-selves,   hum - ble our-selves   and   pray;   Lord, we

give our sin and heal our bro-ken land. 2. Lord, we

C Bm7 Am7 G/B 3 C G/C Am/D C/D Gsus G

✛ CODA rit. and decresc. *"America, the Beautiful"
a tempo

land. O beau-ti-ful for men of faith Who

G E♭ D♭/E♭ E♭7 A♭ E♭/G E♭m/G♭ E♭m6

rit. and decresc. a tempo

found-ed this great land; Pro-claimed for us, "In God we trust," And

D♭/F D♭/E♭ E♭7 A♭2 A♭ A°7 E♭/B♭

cresc. f

held to God's strong hand. A-mer-i-ca! A-mer-i-ca! God

D/B♭ E♭/B♭ B♭9 B♭ E♭ D♭/E♭ E♭ A♭ B♭m/A♭ A♭ D♭/A♭ E♭7/A♭

cresc. f

70

There Is a Redeemer

Words and Music by
MELODY GREEN
Arranged by Tom Fettke

72

giv - ing us Your Son,_____ And leav - ing Your
Spir - it till the work_ on_ earth is done.
Pre - cious Lamb of God, Mes - si - ah, Ho - ly
One.

How Lovely Are Thy Dwellings

Adapted from Psalm 84

SAMUEL LIDDLE
Arranged by Tom Fettke

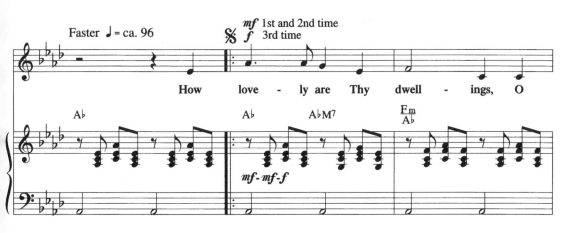

prayer; I would rath - er be a door - keep-er in the

house of my God, than to dwell in the

tents of wick - ed -ness. For a

day in Thy courts is bet - ter than a

Worthy of Worship

TERRY W. YORK

MARK BLANKENSHIP
Arranged by Tom Fettke

The Blessing Song

(A Baby Dedication Song)

Words and Music by
NANCY GORDON,
LINDA WALKER and JAMIE HARVILL
Arranged by O. D. Hall, Jr.

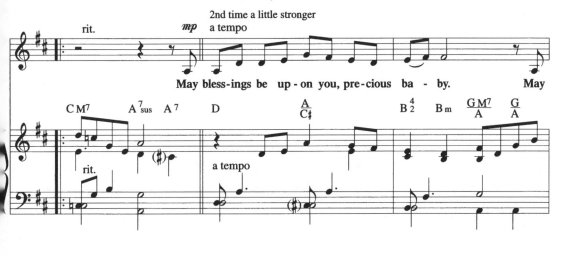

May bless-ings be up-on you, pre-cious ba - by.   May

fa-vor rest up-on your fam-i - ly._____ May your fu-ture be   a

Not Too Far from Here

Words and Music by
TY LACY and STEVE SILER
Arranged by Tom Fettke
and Dennis Allen

92

lose   Not too far___ from___ here. Some-bod-y's for-got - ten how__ to

trust And some-bod-y's dy - ing__ for love   Not too far__ from__

here.   Now I'm let - ting down__ my__ guard   And I'm o -

- pen-ing__ my heart.__ Help me speak__ Your love___ to ev - ery need - ful

I Worship You, Almighty God

with
Holy, Holy, Holy

Words and Music by
SANDRA CORBETT
Arranged by Tom Fettke

How Beautiful

Words and Music by
TWILA PARIS
Arranged by Tom Fettke

102

died, Will - ing to pay the price,____

Dsus D   D/F♯ A7/E D   G2   G   D/F♯

will - ing to pay____ the price.____ 3. How

D/F♯ A7/E D   G2   G   G/A   GM7/A A7 G/A

D.S. al Coda

CODA

Christ.____ 4. How

Dsus   D   D/C   B♭   A♭/B♭

beau - ti - ful-____ the feet____ that__ bring the

E♭   B♭/D   A♭/C   E♭/B♭

104

In the Presence of Jehovah

Words and Music by
GERON DAVIS
Arranged by Tom Fettke

108

The Lord Is My Light

Adapted from Psalm 27

FRANCES ALLITSEN
Arranged by William David Young

Midnight Cry

Words and Music by
GREG DAY and CHUCK DAY
Arranged by Tom Fettke

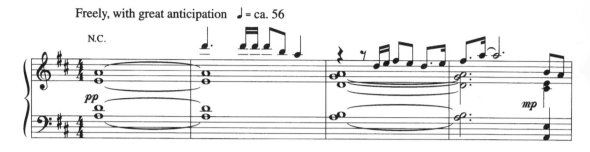

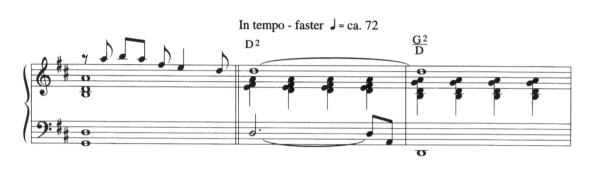

116

The Way of the Cross Led Me Home

Words and Music by
MOSIE LISTER
Arranged by Tom Fettke

voice   soft-ly whis-pered, "Child,__come home."_____   And thro'-

| G♭ | | D♭/A♭ | | E♭m7/A♭ | | A♭ | G♭/A♭ A♭7 |

out   end-less   a - ges   I'll   sing_____ His   praise;   For the

| D♭ | A♭7sus/E♭ D♭/F A♭7sus/E♭ D♭ | D♭/F G♭ D♭/F E♭m7 | D♭/F | G♭ |

way   of the cross,   the old   rug-ged cross,   The__

| D♭/A♭ | G♭/A♭ | A♭ D♭ | G♭ | D♭/F G♭ |

D.S. al Coda ⊕

way   of the cross   led me home._____

| D♭/A♭ | A♭7sus D♭/A♭ A♭9 | Fm/A♭ A♭7 D♭ |

Soon and Very Soon

Words and Music by
ANDRAE CROUCH
arranged by Tom Fettke

Finally Home

DON WYRTZEN
and L. E. SINGER

DON WYRTZEN
Arranged by Tom Fettke

He'll Understand and Say, "Well Done"

LUCY E. CAMPBELL
and KEN BIBLE

LUCY E. CAMPBELL
Arranged by Tom Fettke

Lamb of God

Words and Music by
TWILA PARIS
Arranged by Tom Fettke

1. Your on - ly Son— no sin to hide. But You have
(2. Your gift of) love they cru - ci - fied; They laughed and

sent Him from Your side To walk up - on this guilt - y
scorned Him as He died. The hum - ble King they named a

We Trust in the Name of the Lord Our God

Words and Music by
STEVEN CURTIS CHAPMAN
Arranged by Tom Fettke

1. Some trust___ in char - i - ots, We trust in the name of the Lord our___ God.
2. Some trust___ in the work they do, We trust in the name of the Lord our___ God. 'Cause

Some___ trust___ in hors - es, We trust in the name of the Lord our___God.
by His grace___ all the work is thro', We trust in the name of the Lord our___God.

Beyond the Cross

Words and Music by
MOSIE LISTER
Arranged by Tom Fettke

1. Need-ing strength for my jour-ney___ I knelt at the

(2. Then I) sought re-as-sur-ance and I went to the

cross Where Je-sus once died for me.___ And I

tomb To the place where His bod-y once lay.___ And I

asked, "Is this a place where hope a - bides?" And
cried, "Lord, help me see– is there hope here for me?" And

this He said to me: "Be -
this I heard Him say: "Be -

yond the cross is a tomb that is emp-ty. You

Jesus, the Light of the World

GEORGE D. ELDERKIN
and KEN BIBLE

GEORGE D. ELDERKIN
Arranged by Tom Fettke

150

Give Thanks

Words and Music by
HENRY SMITH
Arranged by Tom Fettke

I Will Be Christ to You

Words and Music by
MARTY PARKS
*Arranged by Tom Fettke
and Marty Parks*

1. All a-lone, dy-ing in-side, Need-ing a com-fort, need-ing a guide. Wound-ed broth-er, bro-ken sis-ter, Look-ing Christ-ward, side by side,

2. By His grace, sealed by His hand, We are a fam-'ly, to-geth-er we stand.

157

159

All Because of God's Amazing Grace

Words and Music by
STEPHEN R. ADAMS
Arranged by Tom Fettke

1. A - maz - ing grace— O how sweet the sound That
(2. Thro') dis - ap - point - ment and— dan - ger, too, Thro'
(3. Then) with the ran - somed a - round God's thone, We'll

saved a poor sin - ner like me! Tho'
la - bors and sor - rows we've come! But
praise our Re - deem - er and King! We'll

once I was lost,_____ yet now_____ I'm found; Tho' I was
God's grace has guid - ed safe - ly thro', And it will
tell how His mer - cy for sin did a - tone; Thro' count-less

G   D⁷/A   G²/B G/B G⁷/B   C   Bm   Am⁷

Last time to Coda

blind - ed,_____ now_____ I see!_____ And it's
sure - ly_____ lead_____ us home!_____
a - ges this song_____ we'll

G/D   A⁹ A⁷ D⁷   G   D

Refrain

all be-cause of God's a - maz-ing grace!_____ Be -

G Gsus/A G/B G⁷/B C CM⁷ F♯/C♯ G/D D/C G/B Bm⁷

163

When I Look into Your Holiness

Words and Music by
WAYNE PERRIN
and CATHY PERRIN
Arranged by Tom Fettke

At the Cross

with
Ten Thousand Angels

ISAAC WATTS
refrain by RALPH E. HUDSON

RALPH E. HUDSON
Arranged by Tom Fettke
and Camp Kirkland

Triumphantly ♩ = ca. 84

He could have called

*"Ten Thousand Angels"

ten thou-sand an - gels

To de-stroy the

world and set Him free.

He could have

174

Reach Out to Jesus

Words and Music by
RALPH CARMICHAEL
*Arranged by Ralph Carmichael
and Tom Fettke*

1. Is your bur-den heav-y as you bear it all a - lone?

Does the road you trav-el har-bor dan - ger yet un - known?

Are you grow-ing wea-ry in the strug - gle of it all?

176

Reach out to Je-sus, He's reach - ing out to you.

2. Is the life you're liv - ing filled with

sor - row and des - pair? Does the fu - ture

press you with it's wor - ry and its care?

178

Jesus, Lord to Me

Words and Music by
GREG NELSON and
GARY MCSPADDEN
Arranged by Tom Fettke

Here We Stand

KEN BIBLE

TOM FETTKE

With great confidence ♩ = ca. 69
A♭2
Freely
mf
F4/2
Fm
E♭/G
F/A
B♭m7
rit.
In tempo
mp 1. The Church was weak and truth was lost in
mf 2. And still to - day the world is lost in
Fm/E♭
D♭/E♭
E°7
F2(no 3rd)
rit.
In tempo
deep and e - vil dark - ness.
deep and e - vil dark - ness.
A low - ly monk was cir - cled by the
And Chris - tians are en - cir - cled by the
D♭6/9
F2(no 3rd)

184

186

Where the Spirit of the Lord Is

Words and Music by
STEPHEN R. ADAMS
Arranged by Tom Fettke

seen on ev-ery hand; Like a gen-tle breeze from heav-en, Like a

breath of love and care, God is pour-ing out His bless-ings on His

chil-dren ev-ery - where. Where the

Spir - it of the Lord is, there is peace; Where the

Spir - it   of the Lord is,   there   is   love.   There is

A⁹   A°⁷   A⁷   A¹³   A⁹   D   D/A

com-fort   in life's dark - est *hour.__There is light   and life; there is help and pow-er in the

Am⁷   DM⁹   G²   C⁹

slight accel.   mf

Spir - it,   in the Spir - it   of the Lord.   Where the

D   Bm⁷   Em⁷   A⁷   D   D/C   B♭⁷   A♭/B♭   B♭⁷

slight accel.

Slightly faster ♩ = ca. 72

Spir - it   of the Lord is,   there   is   peace;   Where the

E♭   E♭°⁷   E♭   B♭m⁶/D♭   C⁷   C+   C⁷/E♭   Fm

mf

*two syllables

191

*two syllables

Arise! Shine!

Words and Music by
ROBERT STERLING and
CHRISTOPHER MACHEN
Arranged by Tom Fettke

1. Lift up your eyes_____ to the heav - ens and see the
2. Look up and see_____ in the light of His face our

light of His king-dom and crown. Lift up your voice_____ to the
hope of the glo - ry to be. Heav-en, the gift_____ of His

Sav - ior and sing, His glo - ri-ous praise we will sound. Stand and be
mar - vel-ous grace, for - ev - er with Je - sus, the King.

count - ed, Je-sus the Sav - ior pro-claim. An - gels sur -

Playing Games at the Foot of the Cross

Words and Music by
MIKE HARLAND
Arranged by Tom Fettke

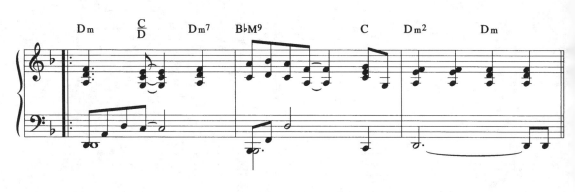

1. You've heard the sto-ry_____ man-y times be-fore,

2. We're so quick to judge them,_____ yet so slow to see

How the sol - diers gam-bled for the robe of the Lord. Their laugh - ter drown-ing out the Sav - ior's cry:

How their games re - sem - ble ones played by you and me. As we fight for po - si - tion in the church of God,

198

So close to His strug-gle, yet so far from the cost. Nev-er feel-ing the shame and nev-er sens-ing the loss,

rit.

2nd time to Coda

1. They were play-ing games
2. We're just play-ing games

rit.

200

for Paulo Barros
Moment by Moment

KEN BIBLE and
DANIEL W. WHITTLE

MAY WHITTLE MOODY
Arranged by Tom Fettke

202

He Is Risen, He Is Lord

Words and Music by
CHRISTOPHER MACHEN
Arranged by Camp Kirkland
and Tom Fettke

206

207

Worship the Lord

Sovereign Lord
Adoration

Arranged by Tom Fettke

210

ho - ly name, Sov-'reign Lord. Sov-'reign Lord.

Faster, but with freedom ♩= ca.80

*"Adoration"

mp 1. Wor - ship the Lord in the beau - ty of ho - li-ness!
mf 2. Fear not to en - ter His pres - ence in pov-er - ty,

Bow down be - fore Him, His glo - ry pro - claim. With
Bear - ing no gifts to pre - sent as your own. Bring

*Words by John S.B. Monsell and Ken Bible; Music by Tom Fettke. Copyright © 1985, arr. © 1999 by Pilot Point Music (ASCAP).
All rights reserved. Administered by The Copyright Company, 40 Music Square East, Nashville, TN 37203.

All in the Name of Jesus

with
Take the Name of Jesus with You

Words and Music by
STEPHEN R. ADAMS
Arranged by Tom Fettke

Freely ♩ = ca. 69
N.C.

mf
mp rit.

In tempo ♩ = ca. 84

1st time:
mp
1. Truth and beau-ty,_____ hap - pi -

2nd time:
mp
2. Care and com - fort, heal - ing and

F/G   G9   CM7   FM7   CM7

ness,   It's all   in the name   of   Je - sus._____

grace–   It's all   in the name   of   Je - sus._____

FM7   C   Gm6/Bb   A7♯5   A7   D2/4 Dm

214

215

*"Take the Name of Jesus with You"

Sweet Beulah Land

Words and Music by
SQUIRE PARSONS

Tenderly ♩ = ca. 80

mp

I'm kind of

home - sick for a coun-try_____ To which_I've

nev - er been be-fore; No sad good-

217

220

Lord of All

Words and Music by
PHILL MCHUGH
Arranged by Tom Fettke

depths where fear would tear such faith a - part. Lord of all of the
vi - sion for each need in life and death. Lord of all of the

na - tions quick to an - ger; bear - ing arms. Lord of all of each
turn - ing of the sea - sons of the earth. Lord of all of the

child held by its moth - er safe from harm.
love that pur-chased man a sec - ond birth.

Lord of all of all seen and un - seen things, of the

He Came to Me

with

He Giveth More Grace

Words and Music by
SQUIRE E. PARSONS, JR.
Arranged by Tom Fettke

sin, _____ He came to me when I pos-

sessed no hope with-in; _____ He picked me up and drew me

gen - tly to His side, _____ And now to-

day in His sweet love I now a - bide. _____ His

228

*"He Giveth More Grace"

The Joy of the Lord

Words and Music by
TWILA PARIS

The Weight of the Cross

Words and Music by
CHRISTOPHER MACHEN
Arranged by Camp Kirkland and Tom Fettke

now would cru - ci - fy.   The   laid   a   cross up - on His back,—and
ob - ject of___ their scorn.   He   nev - er spoke a   word to them,—the

Gm6/D   Em7

pushed Him up___ the road.   The   path would lead___ to Cal - va-ry-___ He
si - lent Lamb__ of God,   This   Man of sor - row bore the cross;__ He

A/B   Bm   Em4   D2/F#

cresc.

cresc.

mf   rit.   mp   a tempo

fell be-neath_ the load._____   And as   I watched I un-der-stood_ the
chose to car - ry on._____   But some-how in His eyes I saw__ a

G2   A sus   A G/A A A/G   G

mf   rit. ⎯⎯⎯   mp a tempo

cresc.

bur - den that__ He bore_____   Was more than just a   heav - y tree;__ the
love be - yond__ the pain,_____   As   if   He knew His sac - ri - fice__ and

A/G   G   A/B   Bm

cresc.

God Will Make a Way

Words and Music by
DON MOEN
Arranged by Tom Fettke

God will make a way where there seems to be no way. He works in ways we can-not see;

Lord, from Your Hand

KEN BIBLE

English Folk Melody
Arranged by Tom Fettke

wine.
blood."
grief!

You serve for - give - ness for my___
I see the mer - cy in Your___
I see You suf - fer as You___

E
G#
A sus   A   D   G M7

need.
eyes,
die.

You serve Your ho - ly life for
I see the pain,___ I see the
I hear You pray:___ It is for

D   G M7   D2/F#   D/F#   D sus/E   G/A

1, 2

mine.
love.

3   cresc.

mf 2. Now from Your   Me.
mf 3. I   see the

D   A sus   A   G/A   A   D   D/C

rit.   f   a tempo

4. O   Je - sus,   Sav - ior, Ho - ly

Bb   Bb/Ab   Ab   Bb/Ab   Eb/G   Ab/Bb   Bb   Eb   AbM7

rit.   f   a tempo

244

Far Above Riches

A Mother's Day Canticle

KEN BIBLE
Inspired by Proverbs 31:10-31

TOM FETTKE

246

share.

care.

end.

4. God of all com - fort, foun - tain of bless - ing,

Ev - er lov - ing in all You do.

Thank you for giv - ing far a - bove rich - es,

Child in the Manger

MARY MACDONALD
and KEN BIBLE

THOMAS J. WILLIAMS,
CAMP KIRKLAND and TOM FETTKE
Arranged by Camp Kirkland and Tom Fettke

1. Child in the manger, Infant of Mary,
   Outcast and stranger, Lord of all.
2. Prophets foretold Him, Infant of Wonder,
   Angels have sung His praise above.

252

God Is with Us

Behold, a Virgin Shall Conceive
God Is with Us! Alleluia!

Arranged by Tom Fettke

*"Behold a Virgin Shall Conceive"

*"God Is with Us! Alleluia"

Heaven's Child

Words and Music by
JOEL LINDSEY
Arranged by Tom Fettke

Gesù Bambino

FREDERICK H. MARTENS
and KEN BIBLE

PIETRO A. YON
Arranged by Tom Fettk

Description?? ♩ = ca. ??

1. When
(2. Our)
(3. A-)

blos - soms flow - ered 'mid_ the snows, Up - on a win - ter night____ Was
God_ so pure,_ so high_ a - bove, Is pleased to come_and dwell.____ Come
gain_ the heart_with rap - ture glows To greet the ho - ly night____ That

born_ the Child,_ the Christ - mas Rose, The King_ of Love_and Light.____ The
see_ the mys - t'ry of___ His love; A Child,_Em-man - u - el.____ The
gave_ the world_ its Christ - mas Rose, The King_of Love_and Light.____ Let

an - gels sang,__the shep - herds sang, The grate - ful earth__ re - joiced,_____
One whom time can - not con - tain And mind__ can nev - er trace_____
ev - ery voice__ ac-claim His name, The grate - ful cho - rus swell._____

And at__ His bless - ed birth the stars Their ex - ul - ta - tion
Has touched our lives__ with ten - der hands And shown_a hu - man
From par - a - dise__ to earth He came That we__ with Him might

voiced._____
face._____
dwell._____ O come, let us a -

dore Him,_____ O come, let us a -

mf

dore Him,_____ O come, let us a -

Eb   Eb6   Ebsus/Bb   Ab   Eb   Fm   Eb/G

mf

dore Him,_____ Christ_____ the

Bb/Ab   Eb/G   Fm7   Eb/Bb   Bb7

decresc.

Lord._____

1, 2   rit.   2nd verse optional   *mf*

Eb   Ab2/Eb   Eb   Ab2/Eb   Eb   Ab2/Eb   Eb   Ab2/Eb   Eb   Bb   Cm   G

2. Our
3. A -

decresc.

rit.

3

mp

Ah_____ O come let us a -

Eb   Bb   Cm   G   C   G/C   C   G/C   C   G/C

mp

*Higher note preferred.

The Virgin Mary Had a Baby Boy

Traditional
and TOM FETTKE

Traditional
Arranged by Camp Kirkland
and Tom Fettke

glo - ry, He come down, He come— from the glo - r'ous King - dom.

He come— from the glo - ry, He come down, He come— from the glo - r'ous King-dom.

He come— from the   Oh,   yes, be-liev-er,   Oh,   yes, be-liev-er,

Oh,   yes, be-liev-er,   He come— from the glo-rious King - dom._____

rit.   Slowly

Topical Index

Alphabetical Index